THE AUTHORITY ON™

Inadequate/Negligent Security Claims in Georgia:

The Definitive Guide for Attorneys, Injured Victims, & Their Families

By:

Gary Martin Hays

For more information, please write:
We Published That, LLC
Adam Weart
3068 Breckinridge Blvd
Duluth, GA 30096

Dedication

As you enter the main building for my law firm in Duluth, Georgia, you will see a plaque hanging on the exterior wall to the right of the front door. It is a quote from the book of Proverbs in the Old Testament:

> *"Speak up for those who cannot speak up for themselves, for the rights of all who are destitute. Speak up and judge fairly; defend the rights of the poor and needy."*
> - Proverbs 31:89

When I pass by this sign, it is a reminder to me and my staff of the tremendous opportunity we have to help people – often as they are experiencing the most difficult and trying of times. I dedicate this book to all of those clients – 39,000 + and growing – who have placed their confidence and trust in me and my law firm to help them with their cases.

This book is dedicated to the attorneys and staff at the Law Offices of Gary Martin Hays & Associates, P.C., for all of the hard work that they perform for our clients, but for the manner in which they do that work. They exemplify their care and compassion every time they pick up the phone or meet with a client. None of this would be possible without their assistance, and for that, I am eternally grateful. I appreciate you, your professionalism, and your tireless work for our clients. Thanks for all you do!

I also want to dedicate this book to my wife, Sheri, and our daughters, Audrey, Ashleigh, and Ava. God bless ALL of you for the love and support you have given me!

Gary Martin Hays

Contents

Introduction

Crime occurs every day in all communities. It does not discriminate based on sex, race, national origin, or socioeconomic status. We see it in pretty graphic detail when we turn on the television. We read about it when we pick up the newspaper and we hear about it when we turn on the radio.

Here are some national crime estimates about violent crime in the United States from 2014. These numbers come from the Federal Bureau of Investigation's Uniform Crime Reporting (UCR) Statistics Database which profiles the number of reported indexed crimes.

National Violent Crime Estimates

Population	Violent Crime Total	Murder & Non-Negligent Manslaughter	Legacy Rape*	Revised Rape**	Robbery	Aggravated Assault
318,857,056	1,197,987	14,249	84,041	116,645	325,802	741,291

* Legacy Rape: These estimates were made using the UCR definition of rape, previously known as "Forcible" rape, by the U.S. Department of Justice.

> "Forcible Rape / Legacy Rape: The carnal knowledge of a female forcibly and against her will. Rapes by force and attempts or assaults to rape, regardless of the age of the victim, are included. Statutory offenses (no force used – victim under age of consent) are excluded."

** Revised Rape: This definition was changed in December 2011 by the UCR.

> "Revised Rape: penetration, no matter how slight, of the vagina or anus, with any body part or object, or oral penetration by a sex organ of another person, without the consent of the victim. Attempts or assaults to commit rape are also included: however, statutory rape and incest are excluded."

Georgia Violent Crime Estimates

Population	Violent Crime Total	Murder & Non-Negligent Manslaughter	Legacy Rape*	Revised Rape**	Robbery	Aggravated Assault
10,097,343	38,097	580	2,159	3,048	12,417	22,052

It is important to note that these are estimates. The numbers could be much higher, especially in the categories of rape/sexual assaults.

So, what can you do if you are a victim of a crime in a commercial establishment? What are your rights? And what were the legal responsibilities for that apartment complex or that business to protect you from that criminal act? The purpose of this book is to set forth for victims and their attorneys the remedies that may be available to them in Georgia under our civil justice system.

If you or a family member are the victim of a violent criminal attack, you need someone who is willing to fight to protect you. You need someone who is willing to fight to also get you all the cash and benefits you are legally entitled to receive. Every single client needs an attorney that cares, that will take action, and will listen.

I suppose I learned best how to work with people when tragedy strikes from watching my father. For more than 50 years, he was a United Methodist Minister serving churches in south Alabama and northwest Florida.

He was always there whenever someone needed to talk - never judging, but listening. It's funny how a lot of people just assume preachers only work on Saturdays for weddings and Sundays to preach - while mixing in the occasional funeral. His work never seemed to end. If the home phone wasn't ringing, there was a knock on the door from one of the members of the church or a friend of a friend who was a member that just wanted to talk.

Helping people who have been hurt at work or in a wreck is not a 9 to 5 type job nor commitment. It requires long hours, rolling up the sleeves, and a dedicated work ethic. I am proud to say that we have helped over 40,000 victims and their families since 1993 in their car wreck, workers' compensation, wrongful death, inadequate security, and social security claims. It has been an honor and a privilege to have helped these wonderful people through their trying times. I'm proud of what I do, and I'm thankful that the Good Lord has given me the opportunity to continue to work in this field.

It is my hope that this book will help guide injured victims and their attorneys through the mine fields that can exist in these claims. Some attorneys would never let you peek behind the curtain to see how they handle cases. To me, there are no secrets. I want to share our knowledge with others so they can help make Georgia safer for all of us.

Should you ever have any questions regarding the information contained in this book, please do not hesitate to contact me at Gary@GaryMartinHays.com. If you would like to have my law firm conduct a free, no obligation, completely confidential consultation of your inadequate security claim, please do not hesitate to call. At a minimum, if you don't call us, please call someone - but please call someone who specializes in these cases.

Our toll-free phone number is 1 (888) 934-8100.
Or you can call (770) 934-8000.

One other note:

The information we are sharing with you in this book is general in nature. It is not designed to provide specific legal advice regarding you and your potential claim. The information in this book may or may not apply to your specific case. Nothing can replace a consultation with an experienced attorney to discuss the facts about your particular claim.

Further, should you have any desire to explore pursuing your potential claim, you should not delay as there are various statutes of limitation which could limit or completely bar your claims for recovery should you not pursue the matter in a timely fashion. We are NOT providing you information regarding the specific statute(s) of limitation applicable to your potential claim as this can only be determined after a detailed consultation of your case with an experienced attorney.

By providing you with this information, we are not giving you specific legal advice about your case, nor have we been retained to handle your claim unless you and our firm have entered into a written contract of representation regarding your potential legal claim.

I sincerely wish you all the best!

God bless and be safe,

Gary Martin Hays

The Law Offices of Gary Martin Hays & Associates, P.C.
3098 Breckinridge Boulevard
Duluth, GA 30096

(770) 934-8000
(888) 934-8100

www.GaryMartinHays.com

Chapter 1
What Are Inadequate/Negligent Security Claims?

Inadequate security (or negligent security) claims are a means by which a victim of a crime may seek civil damages against the commercial establishment or business for the entity's failure to protect that person from a foreseeable crime by a third person.

This is based upon the legal theory that the business (the landowner, the property owner) has a duty to offer "reasonable security measures" and to protect lawful visitors upon their property from attacks by a third party. The assumption is that the crime (attack, rape, assault, shooting, stabbing, etc.) could have been prevented, or at a minimum been made less likely to happen, if the business had used reasonable and appropriate security measures.

It is important to note that the victim of a crime does not have a legal right to civil damages just because they were injured on the business's property, or because they were the victim of a criminal act while on the property. The owner must owe some kind of legal duty to the person on their property. Georgia law has three (3) different classifications for visitors upon a property:

(1) Invitee:

O.C.G.A. Section 51-3-1 sets forth the duty that the owner or occupier of land has to an **invitee** upon its property:

> "Where an owner or occupier of land, by express or implied invitation, induces or leads others to come upon his premises for any lawful purpose, he is liable in damages to such persons for injuries caused by his failure to exercise ordinary care in keeping the premises and approaches safe."

The statute specifically addresses one to whom the owner of the business/property owes the legal duty – **an invitee** – by either express invitation or an implied invitation. An invitee could be a customer that comes onto the property to do business with the store owner. It could also be someone who goes to a restaurant for a meal, or a person that walks through the doors of a motel or hotel seeking to rent a room for the night. As an invitee, as someone who is "invited" onto the property to conduct business, the property owner owes the highest level of protection under Georgia law.

(2) Licensee:

O.C.G.A. Section 51-3-2 sets forth the duty that the owner or occupier of land has to a **licensee** upon its property:

> "(a) A licensee is a person who:
>
> > (1) Is neither a customer, a servant, nor a trespasser;
> > (2) Does not stand in any contractual relation with the owner of the premises; and
> > (3) Is permitted, expressly or impliedly, to go on the premises merely for his own interests, convenience, or gratification.
>
> (b) The owner of the premises is liable to a licensee only for willful or wanton injury."

Licensees are people that are on the property for their own purposes with the express or implied permission of the owner. This could include party guests or social guests - people visiting for their own amusement or enjoyment, or perhaps family friends with an open invitation to visit. Another example may be that of a salesman coming onto the property with the goal of selling something or it could be someone walking inside a store to ask directions or for a restaurant recommendation nearby.

A different duty or standard of care is imposed upon property owners as to licensees. They owe the licensee a duty to warn of a risk of harm if the landowner/business knows of the dangerous condition and the licensee is not likely to be able to discover it.

(3) <u>Trespasser</u>:

A trespasser is someone who comes upon the property of the owner without permission. There is no real duty on the landowner's part to anticipate the presence of a trespasser as one is entitled to assume that other people will obey the law and not trespass on someone else's property.[1] Also, if the landowner is not aware of the presence of the trespasser or of the danger that they may face, there is no duty for the landowner to maintain the property.[2]

It is important to note that there is not a federal law on the books that mandates what legal duties property owners/businesses have to provide security. As previously noted, I shall address this only from the perspective of Georgia law. For the purposes of this book, I shall also only deal with claims that may be presented by the first two categories – Invitees and Licensees.

What types of commercial establishments or businesses can be held liable in an inadequate security claim?

The following is just a list of examples:

- Apartments and apartment complexes
- Colleges and universities – not only in the dorms, but around campus

[1] <u>Norris v. Macon Terminal Co.</u>, 58 Ga. App. 313, 198 S.E. 272 (1938).

[2] <u>Leach v. Inman</u>, 63 Ga. App. 790, 12 S.E.2d 103, at 105 (1940).

- Nursing home and assisted living facilities (claims have arisen from the failure of a nursing home to prevent Alzheimer patients from wandering)
- Hotels, motels, and resorts
- Construction sites
- Parking lots, garages, and decks (including stairwells and elevators)
- Cruise ships
- Hospitals (in-patient molestation by staff or other patients or visitors. Patients are certainly vulnerable while medicated/sedated.)
- Mental health facilities
- Convenience stores (including shootings, stabbings, abductions)
- Bars, nightclubs, and liquor stores
- Movie theaters
- Banks and ATMs (especially when the area is not well lit, or where the person is in an enclosed area without windows to see the entire area)
- MARTA stations and parking lots
- Shopping centers, malls, discount malls, strip malls, retail stores, and outlet malls
- Office buildings, complexes, and parks
- Churches and other places of worship
- Concerts and amphitheaters

Why go after the business or property owner when the third party was the one who committed the crime?

There are several reasons:

(1) Sometimes the criminal is never caught or is unknown.

(2) The crime may never have occurred but for the business not having security, or failing to exercise ordinary care by having proper security measures. In essence, their failure to act or their refusal to properly act allowed the conditions to exist which led to the crime.

(3) It is often rather easy for us to identify the owner or the responsible entity for the management of that

business/premises – especially when the perpetrator is not known.

(4) The owner or responsible entity for that property is often more likely to have insurance that will help pay claims for their negligence.

(5) Pursuing claims against the owners or responsible entities will encourage them and others to have the necessary security systems in place to protect invitees and licensees on their property and will hopefully prevent future attacks.

Who can be held civilly liable in these attacks?

In many claims, there are multiple potential targets, including:

- the criminal defendant, if known;
- the business owner;
- the business tenant, especially if they were contractually responsible for providing security and did not do it, or if their efforts were substandard;
- the management company;
- any security company or contractor that was paid to install, maintain, and/or monitor the security equipment or cameras;
- any security company providing guards that did not properly do their job, or were not properly trained or supervised.

Who can bring the potential claim?

If the victim lives through the attack, is coherent, has the mental/emotional faculties to make an informed decision, and is eighteen (18) years of age or older, then the claim vests with them. If a minor, the parent(s)/custodial parent can bring the claim on the child's behalf.

Some cases may require a guardian be appointed to pursue the claim and monitor any recovery of the victim's behalf, especially if the victim is a child or is mentally incapacitated. Spouses may also have a claim for loss of consortium whenever their partner has been the victim of a criminal attack and suffered injuries.

The purpose of loss of consortium is to compensate the spouse for their loss of "benefits" due to the injuries. This could be based upon loss of love, affection, companionship, comfort, or the damage to the couple's sexual relations because of the attack.

Who has the right to pursue the claim if the victim dies as a result of the attack? The answer will vary depending upon several factors.

Was the victim married? If they were married at the time of the death, then the claim belongs to the surviving spouse.

If the person that died was not married at the time of their death, but was living with their significant other, does this person have a claim for the wrongful death? The answer is NO – because they were not married at the time of the death.

If the victim was not married, then Georgia law holds that if there is no surviving spouse, the claim will vest with the surviving children of the deceased. This will require the Court to appoint someone to handle the claim for the benefit of the child/children.

What are the different types of cases that may arise out of inadequate security claims?

Over the years, we have helped people who have been the victim of the following criminal attacks:

- Assaults
- Sexual assault/rape
- Shooting victims
- Stabbing victims

In all of the claims that we handle, we understand the physical and emotional toll that these attacks can have upon the victims and their families. There is no shame in asking for help to deal with the mental trauma and we work to make sure our clients are able to get the assistance they need to cope with all aspects of their injuries – both physical and emotional.

Chapter 2
What Must You Prove In An Inadequate/Negligent Security Claim?

The victim of a criminal attack can present a negligent/ inadequate security claim based upon the duty imposed on business/ property/land owners for their failure to offer or provide reasonable security measures and to protect invitees and licensees from foreseeable crimes by third parties. The assumption is the crime could have been prevented by the commercial entity – or at a minimum been made less likely – had they used appropriate security measures.

Here is a summary of what we must prove to be successful in these claims:

(1) The victim was authorized or invited to be on the premises at the time of the attack.

(2) The owner of the property owed either a legal or a contractual duty to exercise ordinary care to make the premises safe to the victim. (Or, the owner of the property assumed the duty to provide security but failed to do it in a reasonable and appropriate manner.)

    (3) The property owner failed in its duties (legally or under contract) to provide the victim with reasonably safe premises and did not protect the victim from the criminal actions of a third party.

    (4) The attack – the crime – would not have occurred if the Defendant fulfilled its legal or contractual duty to provide adequate security.

In <u>Ratliff v. McDonald</u>[1], the Court of Appeals held that "[a] property owner is not an insurer of an invitee's safety, and an intervening criminal act by a third party ***generally*** insulates a proprietor from liability unless such criminal act was reasonably foreseeable." (Emphasis supplied.)

But, "[I]f the proprietor has reason to anticipate a criminal act, he or she then has a duty to exercise ordinary care to guard against injury from dangerous characters."[2] If there is no "foreseeability", then there is "no duty on the part of the proprietor to exercise ordinary care to prevent that act" from arising.[3]

So, what are **<u>foreseeable crimes</u>** in Georgia?

One of the ways we may prove that a crime is foreseeable to a business or a property owner is by showing that similar crimes have occurred on or near the property in question so the owner is or should be on notice that more crimes might occur. Evidence of similar criminal activity occurring on or near an owner's property may establish that the crime was "foreseeable."[4]

A crime may be "substantially similar" when a court analyzes the "location, nature, and extent of the prior criminal activities and

[1] 326 Ga. App. 306, 312 (2014).

[2] <u>Days Inn of America v. Matt</u>, 265 Ga. 235 (1995).

[3] Id.

[4] <u>Walker v. Aderhold Props.</u>, 303 Ga. App. 710, 712-713 (2010).

their likeness, proximity or other relationship to the crime in question." [5] However, "substantially similar" does not mean the crimes must be "identical," according to Drayton v. Kroger Co.[6]

The prior incident – the prior criminal act – must be sufficient enough to gain the attention of the business owner so that they might be aware of the dangerous condition which could lead to other attacks, and it is usually a jury question as to whether or not it was reasonably foreseeable.[7]

To further clarify this point, "[f]oreseeable consequences are those which, because they happen so frequently, may be expected to happen again." [8]

It is important to note that you do not always need prior crimes in and around the property to support a claim for inadequate security. In Shoney's, Inc. v. Hudson, the Court of Appeals held that "[A] showing of prior similar incidents on a proprietor's premises is not always required to establish that a danger was reasonably foreseeable. 'An absolute requirement of this nature would create the equivalent of a 'one free bite rule' for premises liability, even if the [proprietor] otherwise knew that the danger existed."[9]

The need to have prior similar incidents as a basis for proving foreseeability was also addressed in SunTrust Banks, Inc. v. Killebrew, when the Court held "[r]equiring a prior similar incident in such cases would lead to arbitrary results, and would engage the

---

[5] Sturbridge Partners v. Walker, 267 Ga. 785, 786 (1997).

[6] 297 Ga. App. 484, 485-486 (2009).

[7] Id.

[8] Medical Center Hosp. Authority v. Cavender, 331 Ga. App. 469 (2015), citing Brown v. Alltech Investment Group, 265 Ga. App. 889, at 894 (2003).

[9] 218 Ga. App. 171, 173-174, 460 S.E.2d 809, cert. denied (1995.)

courts in the mechanistic, unreasoned application of rules, requiring us to turn a blind eye to the simple reality that some business owners may reasonably anticipate criminal activity even if no prior crimes have occurred."[10]

When evaluating the foreseeability of a crime, we look at some of the following factors:

* The condition of the premises when the attack happened. What condition was the apartment, the parking lot, or the business in at the time of the attack? In a state of disrepair? Poor upkeep? Not well maintained?

* Were the security lights out, not working, or non-existent in the area?

* Should the area have better lighting?

* Should brushes have been trimmed or removed to prevent a criminal the opportunity to hide for a surprise attack?

* Did the property have security? Was it 24-hour security? Were the security guards in uniform? Were they patrolling at the time of the attack? Should there have been a security patrol? In car?

* Did the property market "security" and advertise that the apartment community was "gated and patrolled" but there were no security measures in place?

* Were there security cameras in the area? Were they operational? Was anyone watching the cameras or should someone have been watching them?

* Should there be a gated entry? Should it be manned 24 hours?

[10] 266 Ga. 109, 464 S.E.2d 207 (1995)

* One should also look at the nature of the business as there are different security concerns for an apartment complex than there are for a parking lot or a bar.

* Is the business in a low, moderate, or high crime area? And what measures should be put in place for security in light of other prior crimes in the area?

* How many entrances/exits are there to the building and are these controlled? Supervised? Card key or code entrance?

* What kind of door locks or window locks - if any - were used by the apartment complex? The building?

* Were broken windows allowing entrance opportunities? Should security bars have been on the windows to prevent entrance?

* Did the property have a secure perimeter fence? Was it adequate in size/height and in good repair?

* Was there a failure to warn patrons/customers/ invitees/tenants of the prior and/or recurring criminal activity in the area or upon the premises?

* Were security measures recommended but never put in place? Or were they only partially implemented?

* Were security measures upgraded/updated in light of other attacks in the area or on the property?

* Were security measures not implemented because the business was more concerned with profits instead of the safety of the invitees?

* Was there a failure to timely respond or properly respond to the victim of an attack?

* Would reasonable inspection of the premises have revealed the security concerns (broken windows, faulty locks, lights not working, doors, gates, etc., damaged)?

* If the attack was committed by an employee of the business owner/management company, would a pre-employment screening/background check/criminal history have revealed that the person was not fit to work in their job?

* Were there missing master keys? Were there too many duplicated keys? Were keys lost or stolen and the locks not changed?

* Did the business/apartment complex have proper screening procedures for guests on the premises?

* If the company handled cash or were dealing with expensive items (such as jewelry), did the business have proper protective enclosures, pass-through windows, or bulletproof glass to protect the employees or guests?

Often, it is important to hire a security analyst to review the crime scene, as well as the prior crime reports to see if the security measures, if any, that were in force and effect at the time of the crime were adequate under ordinary circumstances.

The following statutes under Georgia law are important ones to review when evaluating and preparing an inadequate security claim:

O.C.G.A. Section 51-3-1:   Duty of owner or occupier of land to invitee

O.C.G.A. Section 51-3-2:   Duty of owner of premises to licensee

O.C.G.A. Section 44-7-14:   Tort liability of landlord

O.C.G.A. Section 51-6-1:   Right of action for fraud accompanied by damage

O.C.G.A. Section 41-1-1:   Nuisance

O.C.G.A. Section 51-12-5.1:   Punitive damages

Chapter 3
Investigating The Inadequate/Negligent Security Claim

The investigation phase is the most critical and important aspect of developing liability against the defendant(s). This is a time where the attorney, the investigators, and the security expert attempt to secure the evidence to demonstrate liability (responsibility) against the business/premises owners or managers. This requires a lot of time and money, including sifting through documents, and talking to witnesses or prior victims.

The following is a step-by-step breakdown that we often follow when investigating these cases:

(1) **Police Incident Report:**

One of the first things that we do is request all police incident reports that were prepared regarding the claim for which we were hired. We are looking for the following:

    *   Information gathered regarding the actual crime. What happened, when, where, who was involved, why?

* Were there witnesses? Any statements from anyone regarding the incident, including the victim and the criminal (if apprehended)? This would include any video or audio recordings.

* Were there any photos or videos recording the crime? Diagrams? Audio recordings?

* Any security camera footage that needs to be preserved/saved/collected immediately? This would include not only the location where the crime occurred, but could also include any adjoining businesses or properties that may have captured the criminal before, during or after the attack.

* Any photos/videos of the scene after the crime? We may also photograph the scene of the crime or the area where the criminal was able to gain ingress/egress to preserve the evidence before alterations/repairs are made.

* Any admissions by the criminal?

* Any admissions by the owner of the property, the manager, or anyone affiliated with the business or with security regarding any failure on their part to protect the victim?

* Any admissions regarding their knowledge of prior crimes in the area?

* We also may speak with the responding police officer and work with any detectives that continue to investigate the crime.

* We may also canvas the area of the crime and speak with other tenants at the apartment complex or other business owners regarding their knowledge of crimes in the area, our potential claim, as well as their security measures that were in force and effect.

(2) **Other Prior Crimes:**

We will also request police reports or initial offense reports for crimes within a given mile radius of where our incident occurred for a specified period of time. Some jurisdictions may have "crime grids" prepared that summarize the numbers and types of crimes in a given area, perhaps a city or a zip code. We are not only looking for similar crimes, but also similar businesses in the area.

For example:

Assume the crime occurred in an apartment complex that did not have 24-hour security. We also find in our search that there were three (3) prior attacks similar to ours just in the last 24 months at this complex. Yet, less than a block away, we find another apartment complex that has 24-hour security and NO attacks/crimes. This could potentially be used as evidence of the reasonable security measures that should have been in place, but were not implemented by the apartment where the attack occurred.

(3) **911 Tapes:**

We secure a copy of any 911 tapes where the actual crime we are handling was reported. We will want to find out who called, what they may have witnessed, and what was said. These tapes often have critical information that allows us to further investigate the claim. We may interview the person(s) that called 911 again for follow-up questions/information regarding the incident.

We may also secure copies of other 911 calls to see if there is any other important information that can be gained through listening to those tapes. Do any of the people reporting those other crimes mention that this is a "high crime" area and this was not the first time they had to call to report a stabbing, a shooting, or a rape?

(4) **Former Victims:**

We may also call and personally interview prior victims of crimes/similar crimes in the area where our attack occurred – especially if the victim was/is a resident of the complex where the crime happened. This may require investigators to help track down these prior victims due to apartment tenants being somewhat transient. These victims may not be allowed to talk as they are currently in litigation over their claim. This will allow us the opportunity to potentially work with their attorneys or the prosecuting attorneys (if criminal charges have been filed) to help develop our claim.

(5) **Surveillance:**

Experienced private investigators in this arena are worth every penny. They may help us conduct surveillance to see if the apartment complex/business actually has 24-hour security, or whether or not they make scheduled patrols around the area. The businesses may claim that they do this religiously but these are facts that must be verified.

(6) **Prior Employees:**

If there have been prior crimes at the business location, you will want to interview, if possible, the victims of those crimes. One often overlooked additional source of information could be employees that worked at the location at the time of those previous attacks. Through discovery, you can ask for a list of all employees who worked at the location for a period of time preceding the incident. You can cross check this with the payroll records that you also request.

If they are no longer employed, then you should be able to locate and interview them regarding the details of the attack and the condition of the premises at the time of the incident. These prior employees may also know of other attacks that were never officially reported to the police. We have found these people to be more forthcoming than those who are current employees at the location as they seem to be concerned about keeping their jobs.

(7) **Police/Detectives:**

Any law enforcement officials that were there on the scene of the attack, or were charged with investigating the incident and interviewing witnesses or the perpetrator(s) should certainly be interviewed. They may not always put everything in their reports as it may not be necessary to them when proving their criminal claim, but it could be invaluable in your civil claim. If warranted, this could also include talking with the police officers/detectives regarding PRIOR attacks at that location.

Also, be sure to review the physical files of these investigations for any photos, diagrams, charts, etc., that may have been taken to see if there is anything of value for use in your case.

(8) Prior Security Company Employees:

If there has been a change in recent years of security companies charged with monitoring and/or patrolling the premises, it may be worthwhile to find out WHY the company no longer is under contract to do so. What did the employees notice while there? Were there any problems that they were aware of that were not addressed by the business owner?

(9) Criminal Defendant:

The actual perpetrator of the crime may be more willing to talk than one might first realize, especially if they are remorseful and/or the criminal charges have been resolved.

Chapter 4
What Damages May Be Recovered In Inadequate/Negligent Security Claims?

Whenever an attorney handles an inadequate security claim, one must not be focused solely on the monetary damages that the victim may incur. The greatest harm that may be inflicted upon the victim is an emotional one, which may require years of therapy and counseling to help them cope with the attack.

The purpose of this chapter is to address the types of damages that may be pursued in these claims; illustrate the importance of using experts to help the victim deal with the emotional struggles; and show how these experts to help a jury fully understand the devastating psychological wounds that may arise.

Damages could include compensation for:

<u>**Medical Bills:**</u>

- ambulance;
- emergency room physician;
- radiology;
- medical doctors and specialists;
- physical therapy;
- psychologist/psychiatrists;

- rape/sexual assault counselors;
- prescriptions;
- and other expenses for which you may have an invoice/bill.

This is easy to prove as all of these health care providers/ suppliers will issue an itemized statement for the services they provide to our clients.

Lost Wages:

If someone misses time from work due to the attack, they may be able to recover for their lost wages provided we have proper documentation of the losses. This proof could include:

- a doctor's disability slip;
- a wage verification form signed by the employer;
- a contract of employment or a contract to perform work;
- or tax returns.

FUTURE Medical Expenses:

No one has a crystal ball to tell you everything the future is going to hold for you medically. However, doctors can sometimes tell us to a reasonable degree of medical certainty what they anticipate you will incur should you eventually need a surgery or have to undergo some additional tests. We will often secure a narrative from your treating physician(s) wherein they set forth future anticipated medical needs/procedures, as well as the projected costs for these items.

Please note: insurance companies do not evaluate your case based upon speculation as to what "may" happen, but upon items that may reasonably be proven through expert testimony.

FUTURE Lost Wages:

The way a jury measures future lost income is for them to determine what the plaintiff would otherwise have earned in his job or profession *but for* the injury. The future lost earnings cannot be speculative and you must have documentation to substantiate your claims. Depending upon the nature or location of the attack, or the severity of the injuries, future lost wages are almost a certain reality. Sometimes it may be necessary to hire an economist to calculate these future lost wages, or at a minimum, the diminished capacity for the victim to earn in the future.

Punitive Damages:

Sometimes the defendant's conduct in allowing the attack to occur are so egregious that the law allows us to seek additional damages known as punitive damages. The ability to pursue these damages are certainly fact intensive. The purpose of punitive damages is to punish, penalize, or deter the defendant from repeating the conduct. Georgia courts have allowed punitive damages in inadequate security claims in Georgia.[1]

> Pursuant to **O.C.G.A. Section 51-12-5.1(b)**:
>
> "Punitive damages may be awarded only in such tort actions in which it is proven by clear and convincing evidence that a defendant's actions showed willful misconduct, malice, fraud, wantonness, oppression, or that entire want of care which would raise the presumption of conscious indifference to the consequences."

General Damages:

These are designed to compensate an injured victim for losses such as pain and suffering, emotional suffering, hardship, or inconvenience.

There is an old saying: "[T]he easiest pain to bear is someone else's." There is a lot of truth to that statement. It is a challenge to get a jury to understand the degree of pain and suffering someone

---

[1] TGM Ashley Lakes, Inc. v. Jennings, 264 Ga. App. 456, 590 S.E.2d 807 (2003). See also Read v. Benedict, 200 Ga. App. 4, 406 S.E.2d 488 (1991); Doe v. Briargate Apartments, Inc., 227 Ga. App. 408, 489 S.E.2d 170 (1997); and Carlock v. Kmart Corp., 227 Ga. App. 356, 489 S.E.2d 99 (1997).

experiences because of an attack – especially when the injuries are not (or may no longer be) visible.

Use of Experts:

A violent, criminal attack may have lasting effects upon a victim. They often struggle with the question "Why did this happen", or "Why did this happen to me?" The emotional damage can be further compounded if the attacker/perpetrator showed uncontrollable anger and violence towards the victim – who, in most cases, was someone they did not even know. The victim may relive the incident time and time again, or they could be petrified with fear that it could happen again. They may also feel humiliated after the attack, embarrassed, shamed, or degraded.

Sexual assault victims can also have other lingering concerns, such as a fear of becoming pregnant, or being infected with AIDS or a venereal disease. Nightmares, insomnia, depression, irritability, or changes in personality are all possible reactions from the victim. Another response that we see from sexual assault victims is the inability to have and enjoy normal sexual relations with their partner. They may feel guilty that they allowed the attack to occur, or shame and humiliation from being the victim of the attack.

The violent, sexual attack can have long-term effects on the victim:

*   94% of women who are victims of rape experience symptoms of post-traumatic stress disorder (PTSD) during the two weeks after the attack.[2]

[2] D.S. Riggs, T. Murdock, W. Walsh, A prospective examination of post-traumatic stress disorder in rape victims. Journal of Traumatic Stress 455-475 (1992).

* Nine (9) months after the rape, 30% of women continue to report symptoms of PTSD.[3]

* 33% of women who are raped contemplate suicide, while 13% of women who are raped actually attempt suicide.[4]

* The potential for drug use post attack is also heightened as the victims of sexual assault are 3.4 times more likely to use marijuana, six (6) times more likely to use cocaine, and ten (10) times more likely to use other major drugs.[5]

The victim is certainly capable of providing details about how the attack has left them emotionally and psychologically devastated. The spouse, significant other, as well as family and friends can help paint a vivid "before and after" picture for the jury about the lasting effects of the attack. A final way to provide proof to a jury can come from medical professionals that have examined, treated, and counseled the victim.

Experts who can help provide insight for the jury include:

- Rape crisis counselors
- Treating physicians
- Psychiatrists
- Psychologists
- Social workers
- Ministers/clergy
- Therapists

[3] J.R.T. Davidson & E.B. Foa (Eds) Posttraumatic Stress Disorder: DSM-IV and Beyond. American Psychiatric Press: Washington, DC (pp. 23-36).

[4] DG Kilpatrick, CN Edumuds, AK Seymour. Rape in America: A Report to the Nation. Arlington, VA: National Victim Center and Medical University of South Carolina.

[5] Id.

These witnesses can discuss everything from the violence and trauma of the actual attack, to the steps that were taken to help the victim cope with the physical and emotional injuries. It is extremely important to show the difference between the need for any pre-attack counseling for any other reason versus the need for counseling after the attack.

Chapter 5
Drafting The Complaint

After a thorough investigation has been completed and the case is viable on liability as well as damages, then a lawsuit should be drafted. For the purposes of this chapter, it is assumed that jurisdiction, venue, etc., all rest in Georgia courts. Furthermore, since these cases are very fact intensive, we shall set forth some of the major allegations that can be made in your complaint rather than trying to create an exhaustive list:

<u>Allegations Against the Building/Property Owner:</u>

(1) <u>Ownership:</u>

It is important to show that the Defendant actually owned the building. This should have been confirmed during your investigation, but it does not hurt to verify.

> * At all times referenced in this instant Complaint, Defendant XYZ CORPORATION was the owner of the building located at 1234 Jones Street, Anywhere, Georgia 30303.

(2) <u>Control</u>:

You will want to make sure that the defendant was in actual control of the premises. If not, then this will alert you to another potential defendant that was charged with operating and/or managing the premises. You will definitely want to secure a copy of any and all leases or agreements where the owner has purportedly relinquished control.

> *   At all times referenced in this instant Complaint, Defendant XYZ CORPORATION operated, managed, maintained, and controlled the building located at 1234 Jones Street, Anywhere, Georgia 30303.

(3) <u>Duty to keep building safe</u>:

Establish that the building owner had a duty to protect invitees (or licensees) from preventable criminal attacks.

> *   At all times referenced in this instant Complaint, Defendant XYZ CORPORATION had a duty to exercise ordinary care in keeping the premises and approaches for 1234 Jones Street, Anywhere, Georgia 30303 safe of people that are on the premises for any lawful purpose.

> *   At all times referenced in this instant Complaint, Defendant XYZ CORPORATION owed a duty to Plaintiff Jane Doe to maintain the premises located at 1234 Jones Street, Anywhere, Georgia 30303, in a condition reasonably safe for the use of anyone lawfully on the property.

> *   At all times referenced in this instant Complaint, Defendant XYZ CORPORATION had a duty to take reasonable precautions as were necessary to protect anyone lawfully on the property located at 1234 Jones Street, Anywhere, Georgia 30303.

(4) <u>Establish Plaintiff was lawfully on the premises</u>:

    *   At all times referenced in this instant Complaint, Plaintiff Jane Doe was lawfully on the premises owned by Defendant XYZ CORPORATION located at 1234 Jones Street, Anywhere, Georgia 30303.

    *   At all times referenced in this instant Complaint, Defendant XYZ CORPORATION owed a duty to Plaintiff Jane Doe to take reasonable precautions as were necessary to protect her while lawfully on the premises located at 1234 Jones Street, Anywhere, Georgia 30303.

(5) <u>Duty to protect from foreseeable criminal acts</u>:

    *   At all times referenced in this instant Complaint, Defendant XYZ CORPORATION owed a duty to Plaintiff Jane Doe to take reasonable precautions as were necessary to protect her while lawfully on the premises located at 1234 Jones Street, Anywhere, Georgia 30303, from criminal acts which were reasonably foreseeable.

(6) <u>Knowledge of Defendant about foreseeable dangers</u>:

    *   Defendant XYZ Corporation knew, or if said entity had exercised reasonable care should have known, that the building it owned, maintained, controlled, and/or managed at 1234 Jones Street, Anywhere, Georgia 30303, and the area in and around said premises, was in a high crime zone with numerous reported criminal attacks upon people in said area.

    *   Defendant XYZ CORPORATION, having possession of this knowledge, or if said entity had exercised reasonable care it would have possessed said knowledge, should have known that criminal attacks were reasonably likely to be committed on people lawfully on the business premises located at 1234 Jones Street, Anywhere, Georgia 30303, unless said

Defendant took reasonable and proper measures to provide:

- adequate security; . . . or
- proper lighting; . . . or
- security fencing; . . . or
- (Insert the appropriate security measure(s) here . . .)

(7) <u>Set forth specific acts of negligence</u>:

Defendant XYZ CORPORATION, by and through its employees or agents, was negligent and breached its duty of reasonable care to Plaintiff Jane Doe, as follows:

* Defendant failed to exercised ordinary care in keeping the premises and approaches safe for Plaintiff Jane Doe at its building located at 1234 Jones Street, Anywhere, Georgia 30303.

* Defendant specifically violated the duty owed to Plaintiff Jane Doe as fully set forth in **O.C.G.A. Section 51-3-1**.

* Defendant failed to provide any security measures for people lawfully upon the subject premises located at 1234 Jones Street, Anywhere, Georgia 30303.

* The failure of Defendant to provide any security measures for people lawfully upon the subject premises located at 1234 Jones Street, Anywhere, Georgia 30303 resulted in the reasonably foreseeable criminal act which was committed against Plaintiff Jane Doe at said time and place.

* Defendant failed to provide reasonable security measures for people lawfully upon the subject premises located at 1234 Jones Street, Anywhere, Georgia 30303.

*   The failure of Defendant to provide reasonable security measures for people lawfully upon the subject premises located at 1234 Jones Street, Anywhere, Georgia 30303 resulted in the reasonably foreseeable criminal act which was committed against Plaintiff Jane Doe at said time and place.

*   Defendant failed to provide any security guards to protect people lawfully upon the subject premises located at 1234 Jones Street, Anywhere, Georgia 30303.

*   The failure of Defendant to provide any security guards to protect people lawfully upon the subject premises located at 1234 Jones Street, Anywhere, Georgia 30303 resulted in the reasonably foreseeable criminal act which was committed against Plaintiff Jane Doe at said time and place.

*   Defendant failed to provide an adequate number of security guards to protect people lawfully upon the subject premises located at 1234 Jones Street, Anywhere, Georgia 30303.

*   The failure of Defendant to provide an adequate number of security guards to protect people lawfully upon the subject premises located at 1234 Jones Street, Anywhere, Georgia 30303 resulted in the reasonably foreseeable criminal act which was committed against Plaintiff Jane Doe at said time and place.

*   Defendant failed to provide an adequate number of security guards that were properly trained to protect people lawfully upon the subject premises located at 1234 Jones Street, Anywhere, Georgia 30303.

*   The failure of Defendant to provide an adequate number of security guards that were properly trained to protect people lawfully upon the subject premises located at 1234 Jones Street, Anywhere, Georgia 30303 resulted in the reasonably foreseeable criminal act which was committed against Plaintiff Jane Doe at said time and place.

* Defendant failed to provide adequate deterrents and other security measures, such as:

  - security locks
  - gated building entrance
  - card key entrance points
  - proper lighting
  - security cameras

  to protect people lawfully upon the subject premises located at 1234 Jones Street, Anywhere, Georgia 30303.

* The failure of Defendant to provide adequate deterrents and other security measures as noted in the preceding paragraph to this instant Complaint at 1234 Jones Street, Anywhere, Georgia 30303 resulted in the reasonably foreseeable criminal act which was committed against Plaintiff Jane Doe at said time and place.

* Defendant XYZ CORPORATION failed to warn Plaintiff Jane Doe, a lawful person upon the premises located at 1234 Jones Street, Anywhere, Georgia 30303, of the fact of and the degree to which criminal acts had been committed at or near the building owned by Defendant.

* Even though Defendant XYZ CORPORATION had superior knowledge of the crimes and criminal acts that had been committed at or near the premises located at 1234 Jones Street, Anywhere, Georgia 30303, Defendant failed to warn Plaintiff Jane Doe of said dangers.

* The security measures that Defendant XYZ CORPORATION had in force and effect at the time and location of this instant incident were inadequate in light of the amount and/or patterns of known

criminal activity in and around the premises located at 1234 Jones Street, Anywhere, Georgia 30303.

* Defendant XYZ CORPORATION had plans for implementing new security measures in and around the premises located at 1234 Jones Street, Anywhere, Georgia 30303, but failed to do so in an effort to save money and increase profits.

* Defendant XYZ CORPORATION had plans for upgrading the existing security measures in and around the premises located at 1234 Jones Street, Anywhere, Georgia 30303, but failed to do so in an effort to save money and increase profits.

* The security systems, alarms, and video surveillance cameras that Defendant XYZ CORPORATION had in and around the premises located at 1234 Jones Street, Anywhere, Georgia 30303 were outdated, defective, broken, inoperable, and in need of repairs.

* The security systems, alarms, and video surveillance cameras that Defendant XYZ CORPORATION had in and around the premises located at 1234 Jones Street, Anywhere, Georgia 30303 were not properly monitored at the time of this instant incident.

* The door locks that Defendant XYZ CORPORATION had in and around the premises located at 1234 Jones Street, Anywhere, Georgia 30303 were outdated, defective, broken, inoperable, and in need of repairs.

* The window locks that Defendant XYZ CORPORATION had in and around the premises located at 1234 Jones Street, Anywhere, Georgia 30303 were outdated, defective, broken, inoperable, and in need of repairs.

* The control entry keypads that Defendant XYZ CORPORATION had in and around the premises located at 1234 Jones Street, Anywhere, Georgia

30303 were outdated, defective, broken, inoperable, and in need of repairs.

* The security gate that Defendant XYZ CORPORATION had for controlling ingress and egress from the premises located at 1234 Jones Street, Anywhere, Georgia 30303 was outdated, defective, broken, inoperable, and in need of repairs.

* The parking lots (walkways, stairwells, hallways, corridors, entrance ways, breezeways) were not illuminated in and around Defendant XYZ CORPORATION'S property located at 1234 Jones Street, Anywhere, Georgia 30303.

* The parking lots (walkways, stairwells, hallways, corridors, entrance ways, breezeways) were not illuminated properly in and around Defendant XYZ CORPORATION'S property located at 1234 Jones Street, Anywhere, Georgia 30303.

* Defendant XYZ CORPORATION did not have any security guard(s) on duty or patrolling the property located at 1234 Jones Street, Anywhere, Georgia 30303, at the time of this instant Complaint.

* Defendant XYZ CORPORATION did not have enough security guard(s) on duty or patrolling the property located at 1234 Jones Street, Anywhere, Georgia 30303, at the time of this instant Complaint.

* Defendant XYZ CORPORATION did not properly train the security guard(s) that was on duty or patrolling the property located at 1234 Jones Street, Anywhere, Georgia 30303, at the time of this instant Complaint.

* Defendant XYZ CORPORATION negligently retained the security guard(s) that was on duty or patrolling the property located at 1234 Jones Street, Anywhere, Georgia 30303, at the time of this instant Complaint.

Allegations Against an Apartment Complex:

In addition to some of the allegations set forth previously against a building owner which could apply to an apartment complex, you could also have the following:

* Defendant ABC Apartment Complex failed to assess and/or appreciate the potential for criminal acts against its tenants, invitees, licensees, and guests at the time of this instant incident.

* Defendant ABC Apartment Complex failed to determine what security measures were necessary to prevent foreseeable criminal acts against its tenants, invitees, licensees, and guests at the time of this instant incident.

* Defendant ABC Apartment Complex failed to implement appropriate security measures which were necessary to prevent foreseeable criminal acts against its tenants, invitees, licensees, and guests at the time of this instant incident.

* Defendant ABC Apartment Complex failed to implement appropriate security measures in response to similar crimes in and around the premises which were necessary to prevent foreseeable criminal acts against its tenants, invitees, licensees, and guests at the time of this instant incident.

* The tenants of Defendant ABC Apartment Complex were not warned about known, specific threats of criminal acts in and around the apartment complex at the time of this instant incident.

* Defendant ABC Apartment Complex failed to have a proper guest/visitor screening system in force and effect at the time of this instant incident which allowed the perpetrator onto the property to commit the crime.

* Because Defendant ABC Apartment Complex failed to have appropriate key control policies or procedures in force and effect at the time of this instant Complaint, Defendant's negligence allowed the criminal (or an employee) to acquire a copy of the key (or master key or key card) which allowed him to gain unauthorized entry to Plaintiff Jane Doe's apartment to commit the attack.

* Defendant ABC Apartment Complex failed to implement appropriate security measures to secure the parking lot for said complex, said actions being necessary to prevent foreseeable criminal acts against its tenants, invitees, licensees, and guests at the time of this instant incident.

* Defendant ABC Apartment Complex failed to remove people that were trespassing upon the premises where the instant incident occurred even though said Defendant was aware of their presence.

* Defendant ABC Apartment Complex failed to remove people that were trespassing upon the premises where the instant incident occurred even though said Defendant should have known of their presence.

Additional claims can arise when the criminal act is committed by an actual employee/agent of the Defendant Owner or Defendant business entity. If the business failed to do a background check on the employee/applicant, or actually completed a pre-employment background/screening check but ignored the findings, potential claims can arise for these acts.

One other area to consider can arise when the Defendant has a security company or patrols trained to respond in the event of an attack, but they either fail to respond, do not respond in a timely manner, or incorrectly respond to the emergency situations. They could be inadequately trained or not properly equipped or unqualified for the security position.

Chapter 6
Drafting The Discovery

After the Complaint has been completed, then detailed, specific Interrogatories, Request for Production of Documents, and Requests to Admit should be drafted. There are certainly some initial, generic questions that should be put forth, but the practitioner is encouraged to not rely on boilerplate language when sending the discovery. Draft pointed detailed questions that apply to your claim to aid you in your investigation and to help narrowly define the issues in dispute.

Again, since these cases are very fact intensive, we shall set forth some of the major questions that could be addressed in these matters:

<u>Interrogatories</u>:

* Who was the owner of the building located at 1234 Jones Street, Anywhere, Georgia 30303, on January 1, 2018?

* What company or entity was in charge of operating, managing, and/or had custody and control over the building located at 1234 Jones Street, Anywhere, Georgia 30303?

* Identify all persons who have assisted in the preparation of answers to these Interrogatories.

* Identify all persons who have any knowledge regarding any facts that have been alleged in Plaintiff's Complaint, as well as all persons who have any knowledge regarding any facts that support any defenses and/or denials in Defendant's Complaint.

* For each such person identified in the preceding Interrogatory, please state:

    (A) The location where each witness was at the time he or she saw, heard, or learned about the alleged occurrence;
    (B) The substance of all information or knowledge about the alleged occurrence known to each such person;
    (C) Whether or not each such person gave any statement or account, either oral or in writing, of his or her knowledge of the alleged occurrence, and if so, give the substance of same.

* State whether you or anyone acting on your behalf obtained statements in any form from any person with knowledge of the incident complained of in Plaintiff's Complaint. If any statement in any form was obtained, state the name and address of the person by whom and to whom such statement was made; the date the statement was made; the form of the statement; and the names and address of all persons presently having custody of the statement.

* Please state whether you or persons subject to your control have any photographs, video tapes, or movies of the incident from the subject matter of this litigation, the scene of the incident, or of the Plaintiff and/or the perpetrator. If the answer is in the affirmative, please state the number of such photographs, video tapes or movies, and the subject of each; the date each was taken; the name and address of the individual who took the same; and the custodian of each photograph or video tape.

* State the name, address, occupational title, and present whereabouts of each person whom you expect to call as an expert witness at the trial of this case, and with respect thereto, please state the following:

(A) the subject matter upon which the expert is expected to testify;

(B) the substance of the facts and opinions to which the expert is expected to testify;

(C) a summary of the grounds for each opinion to which the expert is expected to testify; and

(D) the date and title of any and all reports or other written materials or letters or any other communication of any kind whatsoever that has been generated by each such expert for this case.

* For all documents and things responsive to any of Plaintiff's Request for Production of Documents that you contend is protected from disclosure by any privilege and/or objection, describe the document by providing the following information:

(A) The date of the document;

(B) The author and recipient;

(C) The subject of the document; and

(D) The privilege asserted and/or objection made.

* Please identify each and every paper and electronic document, video, audio, or photograph regarding the Plaintiff's claim which has been destroyed or deleted, and state the date and reason for the destruction or deletion.

* Identify the person, company, or entity that was charged with the responsibility of keeping the premises and approaches for 1234 Jones Street, Anywhere, Georgia 30303 safe for people who are on the premises for any lawful purpose at the time of this instant incident; in addition, please state whether a contract or agreement or memoranda of understanding exists memorializing this.

* Please identify any company or entity that has provided property management services for the premises located at

1234 Jones Street, Anywhere, Georgia 30303 for the five (5) years preceding this incident, including the date of incident. In addition, please state whether a contract or agreement or memoranda of understanding exists memorializing this.

* Please state all actions and precautions that were taken to protect all people that were lawfully on the premises located at 1234 Jones Street, Anywhere, Georgia 30303 for any lawful purpose at the time of this instant incident.

* Please identify all crimes known to this Defendant that occurred within the last 5 years from the date of this instant incident within a 5-mile radius of the premises located at 1234 Jones Street, Anywhere, Georgia 30303.

* Please identify all crimes, attacks, assaults, robberies, muggings, rapes, sexual assaults, or other criminal act that has occurred at the premises located at 1234 Jones Street, Anywhere, Georgia 30303.

* Please state all steps that were taken to investigate ABC Security Company prior to hiring the company to provide security for the subject premises located at 1234 Jones Street, Anywhere, Georgia 30303 at the time of this instant incident, and identify the person(s) who was charged with the task of investigating said security company.

* Please identify ALL security measures which were in force and effect at the subject premises located at 1234 Jones Street, Anywhere, Georgia 30303 at the time of this instant incident.

* Please identify ALL warnings which were provided to any guests, invitees, and licensees regarding prior criminal acts which had been committed at or near the building owned by Defendant XYZ CORPORATION in the 120 days preceding and including the date of this instant incident.

* Please identify ALL security measures that were recommended to Defendant XYZ CORPORATION to implement at the location of this instant incident in and around the premises located at 1234 Jones Street, Anywhere,

Georgia 30303 at any time whatsoever; in addition, please identify the person(s) or entity that made these recommendations.

* Please identify any and all persons, companies, or entities that recommended security measures and/or performed a security audit to Defendant XYZ CORPORATION to implement at the location of this instant incident in and around the premises located at 1234 Jones Street, Anywhere, Georgia 30303 at any time whatsoever.

* Please identify all security systems, alarms, and video surveillance cameras that Defendant XYZ CORPORATION had in and around the premises located at 1234 Jones Street, Anywhere, Georgia 30303 at the time of this instant incident, including the location of these items, as well as any and all locations where these items were monitored.

* Please identify all control entry keypads that Defendant XYZ CORPORATION had in and around the premises located at 1234 Jones Street, Anywhere, Georgia 30303 at the time of this instant incident, and state their exact locations.

* Please identify all the location of all security lights, if any, in and around the premises located at 1234 Jones Street, Anywhere, Georgia 30303 at the time of this instant incident.

* Has this Defendant ever had a claim presented or a lawsuit filed against it for failing to provide adequate security or safety measures at any time whatsoever? If so, please identify the nature of the claim(s), the facts regarding the claim(s), and the identity (including full name, address, and phone number) of the person(s) making the claim(s).

Request for Production of Documents:

Pursuant to **O.C.G.A §9-11-34**, you are requested to produce for inspection and copying the following documents in your possession, custody, and control:

*   All letters, memoranda, and other forms of written communication(s) to or from any person, firm, corporation, or any other entity relating in any way to the processing of this instant claim.

*   All written records of any oral communications, whether in person or by telephone, to or from any person, firm, corporation, or any other entity relating in any way to the processing of the claim noted above.

*   All written records of any investigation conducted in connection with the claim noted above.

*   All other written documents pertaining to Plaintiff and the claims at issue in this instant action.

*   All records, documents, statements, or any other materials of any kind whatsoever prepared by, secured by, and/or reviewed by you, or any of the insurance company's subsidiaries or parent companies, prior to hiring an attorney to represent the Defendant in this instant action.

*   All photographs of any person, place, or thing that has any relation whatsoever to the claims being made in this action.

*   All photographs of the scene where this instant incident occurred.

*   All photographs of any individual involved in this instant incident.

*   Please produce all statements or reports (written, typed, or otherwise) made by any person concerning the occurrence complained of taken by you, at your direction, or by anyone affiliated with you or any of said company's subsidiaries or parent companies involving this instant action.

*   Please produce a copy of any incident report, memorandum, or recorded account of any kind or by any name whatsoever relative in any way to the incident which forms the basis of Plaintiff's Complaint in this instant action.

*   Please produce copies of any and all internal reports or investigations done by or on your behalf prior to hiring an attorney regarding this instant action.

*   Please produce all reports prepared by any and all experts retained or consulted by or on your behalf, or any of the insurance company's subsidiaries or parent companies, secured prior to hiring an attorney, regarding any aspect of Plaintiff's claims in this instant incident.

*   Please produce any and all experts' reports which have been prepared in connection with this instant action on your behalf, or any of the insurance company's subsidiaries or parent companies, prior to hiring an attorney.

*   Please produce any report of investigation from any governmental agency or private organization, company, individual, or entity relating to the occurrence in question.

*   Please produce all purchase invoices, repair estimates, appraisals, and documents establishing the cost of any repairs and/or modifications that needed to be made to Defendant's premises BEFORE this instant incident occurred.

*   Please produce ALL requests for repairs, including any customer (tenant) requests and/or complaints, that needed to be made to Defendant's premises in the one (1) year BEFORE this instant incident occurred.

*   Please produce all purchase invoices, repair estimates, appraisals, and documents establishing the cost of any repairs and/or modifications that were made to Defendant's premises AFTER this instant incident occurred.

*   Please produce copies of all correspondence, letters, memoranda, or other written records or documents provided by you or anyone at your direction to any witness or purported witness to this incident; to any expert, to any judicial, governmental, or quasi-governmental agency, body, group, or organization contacted with regard to this occurrence; and to any police officer(s) and/or detective(s) that investigated this instant incident.

* Please produce any and all reports from any security experts regarding this instant incident.

* All letters, memoranda, and other forms of written communication and written records of oral communications, whether in person or by telephone, referring or relating in any way to the issuance of the policy of insurance at issue in this instant action, including any application(s) for insurance.

* All documents relating in any way to any claims that were made against this Defendant for any claims of failure to provide a safe premises.

* A complete copy of all records and documents in your possession concerning any prior claims, any prior lawsuits, and any prior statements regarding crimes committed at the Defendant's premises for the five (5) years preceding this instant incident.

* All settlement agreements entered into by you with any person or entity regarding any prior incidents as referenced above.

* A copy of all reports or statements filed or filled out by you concerning any incidents relevant to this lawsuit.

* All written communications and written records of oral communications, whether in person or by telephone or e-mail, between any employee of defendant and any third party relating in any way to the claims at issue in this action.

* All manuals, memoranda, directives, letters, and other forms of written communication directed to any employee of this Defendant, or any other person acting on behalf of Defendant that refer or relate in any way to this instant action. If, in responding to this request, you withhold production of these documents on the ground of any

privilege not to disclose the document, please state with respect to each such document:

1. The type of document involved and a general description of the contents of the document;
2. The name, business and residence addresses, phone numbers, and position of the individual from whom the document emanated;
3. The name, business and residence addresses, phone numbers, and position of the individual to whom the document or a copy of the document was sent;
4. The date of the document;
5. The privilege upon which you rely in withholding the document;
6. The names, business and residence addresses, phone numbers, and positions or occupations of individuals known or believed by Defendant to have knowledge concerning the factual basis for Defendant's assertion of privilege with regard to the document.

*   A complete copy of the schedule for any and all employees for the week preceding this incident, including the week of this instant incident.

*   A complete copy of the schedule for any and all security guards, patrols, or other security personnel, including off-duty law enforcement officers, for the week preceding this incident, including the week of this instant incident.

*   A complete copy of any and all security evaluations, audits, or threat assessments performed/conducted by anyone, including employees or agents of this Defendant, and any outside person, consultant, company, or entity – public or private – at any time whatsoever, BEFORE and AFTER this instant incident.

*   A complete copy of all policies and procedures, including prior versions before any changes/additions/amendments were made, regarding safety and security at the Defendant's premises which are the subject of this instant incident.

* A complete copy of all policies and procedures, including prior versions before any changes/additions/amendments were made, which were used to train, and/or provide direction to any security company, security guards, patrol, or law enforcement individual for their work at the Defendant's premises which are the subject of this instant incident.

* A copy of any complaints, letters, or notes regarding any aspect of the Defendant's security, or lack thereof, at any time for the premises which are the subject of this instant incident.

* A copy of any and all marketing pamphlets, manuals, brochures, ads, commercials, or any other document of any kind whatsoever this Defendant utilized to promote, market, and/or advertise its business (or apartment, etc.).

* A copy of any and all documents, videos, photos, screen capture, web capture, or any other tangible item of any matter whatsoever regarding the Plaintiff in this instant incident.

* (Apartment Complex) A copy of the lease agreement between this Defendant and the Plaintiff, including any and all prior versions.

* A copy of any and all agreements with any company, person, or entity to provide security to the Defendant's premises for the five (5) years preceding this incident, through the date of this instant incident.

* A copy of any and all reports, notes, incident reports, accident reports, security logs, patrol logs, audio and/or video tapes, recordings, internal memoranda, correspondence, emails, summaries, witness statements, complaints, security schedules, patrol schedules, bills, invoices, or any other tangible document of any kind whatsoever from any company, person, or entity that provided security to the Defendant's premises for the five (5) years preceding this incident, through the date of this instant incident.

* Any and all files regarding any crime prevention or deterrence plans that were contemplated, discussed, or recommended, as well as any that were implemented in whole or in part at the Defendant's premises for the five (5) years preceding this incident, through the date of this instant incident.

* A copy of any and all documents regarding the oversight, management, maintenance, and repairs for Defendant's premises for the five (5) years preceding this incident, through the date of this instant incident.

* A copy of any blueprint or construction document for any work that was performed or was contemplated being performed at Defendant's premises for the five (5) years preceding this incident, through the date of this instant incident.

* A complete copy of the official personnel file(s) for any employee(s) of this Defendant charged with providing security for Defendant's premises for the five (5) years preceding this incident, through the date of this instant incident.

* A complete copy of the official personnel file(s) for any employee(s) of any security company charged with providing security for Defendant's premises for the five (5) years preceding this incident, through the date of this instant incident.

* A copy of any and all videotapes or DVD's or CD's used for training purposes for your employees regarding safety and security for Defendant's premises for the five (5) years preceding this incident, through the date of this instant incident.

* A copy of any and all videotapes or DVD's or CD's used for training purposes for any employee(s) of any security company charged with providing security for Defendant's premises for the five (5) years preceding this incident, through the date of this instant incident.

*   A complete copy of any and all employee orientation manuals and personnel policies provided to new employees of this Defendant for the five (5) years preceding this incident, through the date of this instant incident.

*   Please produce a copy of any and all documents which would evidence with particularity all training regarding security and safety issues received by the employees of this Defendant for Defendant's premises for the five (5) years preceding this incident, through the date of this instant incident.

*   Please produce a copy of any and all documents which would evidence with particularity all training regarding security and safety issues received by any employee(s) of any security company charged with providing security for Defendant's premises for the five (5) years preceding this incident, through the date of this instant incident.

*   Please produce a copy of any and all documents or any other tangible evidence of any kind whatsoever which you allege shows that this Defendant's conduct met its own policies, procedures, guidelines, standards, rules, regulations, and/or directives to ensure the Defendant's premises where Plaintiff was injured on ***DATE OF INCIDENT *** was in a reasonably safe condition.

*   Please produce a copy of any and all documents or any other tangible evidence of any kind whatsoever which you allege shows that this Defendant's conduct met its own policies, procedures, guidelines, standards, rules, regulations, and/or directives to ensure the Defendant's premises where Plaintiff was injured on ***DATE OF INCIDENT *** would not expose said Plaintiff to unreasonable risks or dangers.

*   Please produce a copy of any disciplinary actions that were taken against any employee(s), contractor, or agent of this Defendant as a result of the incident regarding the Plaintiff which forms the basis of this instant Complaint.

*   The complete file folders in which ALL of the preceding
         documents are kept.

Practice tips:

(1)   ALWAYS review the Defendant's answer when drafting your
         discovery. If there is a **denial** to any allegation, attack it – be
         curious – find out why the Defendant denied this through
         carefully crafted Interrogatories, Request for Production of
         Documents, or Requests to Admit.

(2)   If there is a response that the Defendant "does not have
         sufficient evidence to admit or deny," then carefully craft
         discovery to find out more. Did the Defendant or their
         attorney(s) exercise due diligence in their investigation of
         the claim? Nail them down on the specifics of what was
         done, when it was done, and who did or didn't do it.

(3)   When you receive the responses to your discovery, do not
         just file it away. THOROUGHLY review them. Draft and send
         a good faith letter if the Defendant was not fully
         forthcoming in their responses. If they fail to comply, then
         file the Motion to Compel and Motion for Sanctions.

Chapter 7
Do I Need A Lawyer?

So, you or a family member has been the victim of a violent attack at a commercial establishment, a building, a parking lot, or at an apartment complex. The insurance company for the business tells you there is no need to call a lawyer as they will "Take care of you . . ." Surely this is a claim that you can handle on your own against the insurance company and their lawyers, right?

Please – DO NOT FALL INTO THIS TRAP!!! There are far too many land mines in this claim than you might realize. Here are just a few concerns:

* Are you getting a fair settlement?

* Will you have to repay your health insurance for any amount that they paid to your health care providers? If so, how much?

* If the potential Defendant (or a possible additional Defendant) in your case is a city, county, state, or federal government entity, do you know what and how to send an "ante litem" notice to the Defendant before you can proceed with your claim?

* Do you even know what an "ante litem" notice is or whether or not it applies to your case?

* What statutes of limitation apply to your claim?

* Do you really have a full understanding of what the future may hold for you medically? And did you get a report from your treating physician(s) to include in your demand package?

* If the claim does not settle, have you irreparably damaged your claim to a point where no lawyer wants to step in and handle it for you?

* Will you know what to do if the insurance company is taking their time getting back with you, or worse yet, completely ignores you?

* Do you have the time to collect, decode, and understand all of your medical records and bills from all of your health care providers?

* Are you available at all times during the work day to make calls and wait for return phone calls from the insurance company or your doctors?

* Will you know how to secure eyewitness statements? What if you can't locate that witness? Do you have the ability, time, or resources to locate him/her?

* Are you comfortable talking with your employer or HR department to get the lost wage information in a form that the insurance company will understand and not question?

* Do you know what documentation the insurance company needs to FAIRLY evaluate your claim?

* What if the insurance company's adjuster is out of state?

* What if they ask you to sign a medical authorization that allows them access to your entire medical history?

* Do you give them a recorded statement?

* What if you have no health insurance?

* What if you had a pre-existing medical condition that was aggravated in the incident?

* Do you have the time, the temperament, the patience, and the knowledge to handle this claim on your own?

I'll give you the same advice I would give anyone calling my office about a potential inadequate security/negligent security claim:

Talk with an EXPERIENCED personal injury attorney about the facts of your claim. If they feel you have a potential claim, then hire that attorney.

If it is a claim that I am willing to handle at my law firm, I tell the client:

If you don't hire us, hire someone – but please hire someone that is a specialist in inadequate security/negligent security claims. You have absolutely nothing to lose by hiring us, but think of all you could lose if you don't!

Chapter 8
How Do I Find The Best Lawyer For My Case?

A question I am often asked by people is "How do I choose the best lawyer for my case?"

The hiring of a lawyer is an important decision and can make or break your case in some situations. Here are some tips you can use to help you find the attorney best suited to help you with your claim:

(1) **Find out if the attorney specializes in the area of law in which you need him or her.**

For example: If you are hurt on the job, you don't want to hire an attorney that mainly handles divorce cases or DUI cases. In my opinion, the days of an attorney handling all legal matters from divorces to real estate closings to auto accident claims are long gone. You have heard the old expression: "Jack of all trades. Master of none." I firmly believe this. Laws change constantly. It is very difficult, if not impossible, for an attorney to keep current on the latest happenings in every legal arena.

Attorneys can claim they "specialize" in a certain area of the law, but do your due diligence to verify this. If the attorney claims to specialize in "personal injury" claims, but his/her website lists cases outside the personal injury arena like bankruptcy, or criminal defense, or collection defense matters, then there is a good chance they have not handled or do not handle a lot of cases for car wreck victims.

Inadequate security cases are certainly a unique area of the law within which to practice here in Georgia. This is not an area where an attorney should practice every now and then. Specialization is key! This is also not a claim where you want your case to be the first one in this legal niche that the attorney has ever handled.

(2) **Find out if the attorney is recognized in your field as an expert <u>by other attorneys</u>.**

What awards or honors has the attorney received? For example, I have previously been recognized as a "Super Lawyer" by other lawyers in Georgia. This is an honor given to only the top 5% of attorneys in the state.

Another way to see if the attorney is respected in the field is to find out if he/she lectures to other attorneys around the state in their practice areas. I've taught other attorneys who devote a substantial portion of their practice to personal injury claims on how I handle car wreck, wrongful death, personal injury and workers' compensation claims at my law firm.

I am also a member of the Multi-Million Dollar Advocate's Forum. This is one of the most prestigious groups of personal injury attorneys in the world. Membership is limited only to attorneys who have received a settlement or verdict of at least two (2) million dollars.

(3) **It is also VERY important that the attorney has EXPERIENCE handling your type of claim.**

Find out how many cases the attorney has handled like yours. You do not want your case to be the attorney's first! For example, at the time that I am writing this book, my firm has helped over 39,000 injured victims and their families for cases involving serious injuries and deaths due to car wrecks, workers' compensation claims, inadequate/negligent security cases, nursing home abuse, and defective products or drugs.

(4) How big is the law firm? Including attorneys AND support staff?

I also believe the size of the law firm matters, and not necessarily the number of attorneys the firm has. Let me explain. As attorneys, we are often in court, away from the office taking depositions, or out meeting with experts on our cases. We aren't always available to answer our clients' questions. It is important for the attorney to have a knowledgeable support staff to assist you with your questions when the attorney is not available. It is also important that my attorneys and staff have continuing education in the area in which they practice.

(5) Does the law firm use the latest in technology?

At my law firm, you will not see a big law library because we don't need all of those legal books as all of our legal research is computerized. I have invested hundreds of thousand dollars in state-of-the-art computer hardware and high-tech programs specifically designed to better serve our clients' needs. When you call, we can instantly access your database to tell you what has happened, and what will be happening with your claim. This process allows us to efficiently handle your case and keep you better informed.

Who NOT to Hire!

Over the years, I have provided expert advice on all of the major network affiliates in Atlanta, including ABC, CBS, FOX, NBC, and the CW Network. I also made guest appearances on CNN's Headline News, CNBC, and have appeared on Fox & Friends. I even hosted the only five (5)-day-a-week legal talk show on Atlanta's CW Network, "The Gary Martin Hays Show." As a result of those appearances, I receive countless e-mails from people regarding their potential claims.

I strongly suggest you NEVER hire an attorney that contacts you out of the blue – someone who you have never called or emailed regarding your claim. The same thing applies to anyone acting on that attorney's behalf who are out there engaging in this kind of practice.

We call these people "runners." The goal for these runners is to refer you to attorneys, doctors, or chiropractors to represent them. If the attorney or chiropractor is able to sign up the client, they will pay the runner a referral fee.

This practice is illegal and unethical for attorneys to be out there soliciting cases like this. This practice is called "solicitation." Further, we are ethically prohibited from paying anyone else to solicit an injured victim to hire our office. Attorneys hire these runners to do their dirty work and deny they had any knowledge this person was out soliciting cases for them.

Some runners will refer the injured person to a doctor or chiropractor who will conveniently have an attorney at the office when they arrive for their first visit. The chiropractor will strongly recommend that the injured person sign on with this attorney or they will have to pay for all of their doctor's visits up front. It is a racket and a scam.

What advice do I have if this happens to you? Here are a couple of suggestions:

First: Get the name and phone number of the person that is calling you. Ask them what lawyer they are working with on these cases. If they deny they are working with a lawyer, ask them what doctor.

As soon as you have the name of the runner, the attorney, or the doctor, tell the person calling you that you appreciate the information. You are now going to call the proper authorities and they should not call you again. Hopefully, they will leave you alone after they hear this.

Second: NEVER, NEVER, NEVER hire any attorney or doctor that will solicit you to be their client or patient. It is unprofessional, unethical, and illegal for them to be doing this. Is this the kind of person you want to entrust with your medical care and your legal case?

Everything I do to market and promote my law firm is completely within the rules set forth by the State Bar of Georgia. I let people know that I'm here for them. If they are hurt and have a question about their rights, or the insurance company's responsibilities, I'm just a phone call or an email away.

Attorney's Fees and Costs

I have been practicing law strictly in the personal injury/workers' compensation field for over 29 years. The standard fee contract that attorneys use is called a "contingency fee contract." In layman's terms, this means (or SHOULD mean) that there are NO attorney's fees unless there is a recovery on the claim. You should not have to pay the attorney a retainer, nor do you pay him/her by the hour, the phone call, the letter, etc. But like any other contract, you should read the contract and UNDERSTAND all terms of the contract before you sign it!

Keep this in mind as well: the attorney works for you. If you do not feel he/she is giving your case the attention it needs, then I encourage you to schedule an appointment to meet with him. Make sure both of you are on the same page and timeline about what will be happening on your case and when. There are several great lawyers out there handling workers' compensation and personal injury claims. Not all of them are great at interacting with their clients and keeping them informed about the work that is being done on their file. Err on the side of trying to work things out with your attorney and get your questions answered.

There may be a time when you do not have a good feeling about the attorney or his office staff that is handling your claim. If your efforts to communicate with him through calls and emails go unanswered, and you feel as though your problems are not resolved, it may be time to move on and get an opinion from another attorney. The fee agreement allows you to cancel the contract at any time – and you don't even have to explain your reason(s) to the attorney. You will, however, possibly be responsible for paying the attorney for the reasonable value of the work performed or he may place a lien on the recovery in your case.

When the case settles, the attorney will also seek to be reimbursed for any costs advanced and expenses he incurred while working on your case. Every attorney charges for these costs and they are necessary to gather the material to present your claim to the insurance company or to prepare your case for trial. These expenses could include depositions, office meetings with doctors, narratives, or possibly other experts.

At our law firm, we typically advance these costs for our client and pay the providers and experts for their services. We are willing to wait for a successful conclusion of the claim to get reimbursed. This way, our clients do not have to worry about coming out of pocket for these expenses – especially at a time where they are hurting – physically and financially.

The choice is certainly yours on whether or not you hire an attorney. Remember: you only have one shot at justice to recover all the cash and benefits to which you are entitled. I highly recommend you hire an attorney! Take advantage of the FREE consultation that some attorneys offer. This will allow you the opportunity to talk with the attorney to see if you have a good comfort level with his knowledge of the law, as well as with his ability to interact with you in a genuine, caring, compassionate manner.

Chapter 9
Conclusion

There are three (3) final things I want to stress to everyone that reads this book:

1. **This book is just a starting point for you to learn about your inadequate security claim.**

   Hopefully, it will provide you with the information you need so you can openly discuss the facts and the law as it applies to your claim with your attorney. Remember: No two cases are alike and this book is not and cannot be a "one size fits all" manual that applies to every negligent security case in Georgia. Nothing can replace you taking the time to have the specific facts of your case thoroughly discussed with a lawyer that is experienced in handling inadequate security claims.

2. **For the attorneys that practice wrongful death and personal injury law in Georgia — and do it the right way — I sincerely thank you and applaud you!**

   Thank you for not using runners or for "chasing ambulances." Thank you for taking up the fight to be an advocate for the injured consumer. This battle is truly one between David and Goliath, but it is worth it. This book was written for you just as much as it was for the injured victims. Please read it and use it and give me your feedback. But please understand, no portion of the book can be copied or used in any way without my express, written permission. Should you have any questions, please do not hesitate to contact me.

3. DO NOT TAKE ON THE INSURANCE COMPANY AND THEIR LAWYERS BY YOURSELF!

Please know that if you or a family member are injured in violent criminal attack, rape, shooting, stabbing, or sexual assault due to inadequate security/negligent security at a commercial establishment, parking lot, apartment complex, or other business, you do not have to take on the battle with the insurance company and their lawyers by yourself. You owe it to your family – to yourself – to get the help you need. Our consultations are always free, completely confidential, and there is no obligation.

You have nothing to lose by calling us, but think of all you can lose if you don't! The phone number is (770) 934-8000, or toll free 1 (888) 934-8100. You can also check out our website: www.GaryMartinHays.com. It is loaded with informative videos and articles regarding workers' compensation claims here in Georgia.

God Bless!

Gary Martin Hays

Summary and Example

The following excerpts for inadequate/negligent security is based on segments from my show "Do I Need a Lawyer?". You can view short segments of the show on YouTube by searching for the Law Offices of Gary Martin Hays & Associates, P.C., or by clicking here.

During the show my team and I sometimes fielded legal questions submitted by an audience member before the show. For this section let's consider a question sent by a woman named Margaret from Doraville, GA:

> *Our son-in-law was robbed and then shot and killed in a parking lot of his apartment complex in Atlanta. Our daughter is obviously very upset and so are we. We are also concerned for our two grandchildren -- ages 6 and 4. He only had a life insurance policy through his work for $10,000. This will barely cover the funeral and burial expenses.*
>
> *The apartment where they were living advertises that they have security. You have to have a magnetic card to get through the gate. The guy who shot our son-in-law was not even a resident there. And we have learned that there were other robberies and attacks in the complex too. Do we need a lawyer?*

Wrongful death cases are some of the most difficult cases to handle as an attorney from an emotional standpoint. You learn how much of an impact the deceased had on their family, at work, and in their neighborhood and community.

It is the attorney's job then to show the insurance company or jury what the full value of the victim's life would be.

Let's look at Margaret's question in two parts:

1. **Who has the right to recover for the victim's death?**
2. **Could the apartment complex be liable for not having adequate security to protect its tenants?**

Under Georgia law, the surviving spouse may bring an action for the wrongful death of their spouse. Whenever there are surviving children, the spouse is required to share the proceeds with them of the wrongful death recovery based on whatever compensation the attorney is able to secure through a settlement or verdict. So, the surviving spouse is the one that pursues the claim as an individual and as a representative of the minor children.

Inadequate/negligent security cases are not easy. They are time intensive and very difficult.

There are five ways I try to show the defendant business owner was negligent in protecting people on their property.

5 Ways to Show Business Owner Negligence

1. Prior Crimes
2. The Defendant Business Owner's Internal Reports
3. What Security Practices Are In Place?
4. Prior Victims
5. Security Experts

1. Prior Crimes

This is the most common way to show an apartment complex or other business is liable for these types of incidents by establishing that the business knew or should have known about prior crimes in the area. One way to prove this is by securing crime reports from the local police department through an open records request.

2. The Defendant Business Owner's Internal Reports

Look to see if the defendant business had any internal reports which identified prior crimes in the area as these are admissible as evidence.

3. What Security Practices Are in Place?

Examine what security practices a business has in place to protect the people who are invited onto the property. A standard of care used by similar businesses can be used to show what should be in place to protect others. If the evidence reveals that the neighboring property owners are taking measures which far exceed the defendant property owner's efforts, then we can show this as evidence of the defendant's failure to meet the standard of care in providing security.

4. Prior Victims

Interview prior victims of similar crimes at the property or in the area. The names can be gathered from police reports. This further emphasizes that the business knew of prior security incidents.

5. Security Experts

Security experts may be necessary to establish that the defendant breached the standard of care by not having adequate security.

Here are a few key things to keep in mind when considering an inadequate/negligent security case:

When Attacks Occur...

- The attacker is a resident at the apartment complex, or is the guest of a resident.
- The attacker came onto the apartment complex grounds as a trespasser.

If the Attacker Lived at the Apartment Complex...

- Could the apartment have screened the tenant better?
- Is there adequate lighting at apartment complex?
- Was there a fence? If so, was it broken?

If the Attacker Is a Trespasser...

- Have other attacks occurred (shootings, sexual assaults, and other violent crimes)?
- Did the apartment complex implement reasonable/ necessary safety measures to protect its tenants from previous crimes?

Factors That Could Have Prevented the Crime From Occurring...

- Criminal background checks on existing tenants
- Replacing burned out or broken lights in parking lot or breeze way
- Adequate fencing
- Proper working locks on all doors or windows

Using these tactics, my law firm discovered that there had been 13 armed robberies at the complex within the two years before the victim's tragic death. The apartment was on notice that there was a serious security problem on their premises but they did not do enough to protect the tenants that paid money to live there. The complex failed to take any action to remedy or reduce the danger to its tenants and allowed the dangerous environment on the property to persist.

The case eventually settled for a very high confidential figure when the apartment complex and insurance companies were presented with the evidence.

This case, like so many other premises liability/inadequate security cases, was challenging – and I'm a lawyer! Pursuing justice against a business or insurance company is never easy and certainly not something you will want to do on your own. You need a law firm on your side to back you up – if not mine, then someone else's.

Violent Crime Statistics for Georgia

According to the 2016 Summary Report Uniform Crime Reporting (UCR) Program from the Georgia Crime Information Center, there were 38,893 violent crimes (murder, rape, robbery, and aggravated assault) reported by law enforcement in the state. Violent crimes offenses occurred at a rate of about 355 per 100,000 people and represented about 11.4% of all crime that year.

Nationally, there were an estimated 1,248,185 violent crimes at a rate of about 386.3 offenses per 100,000 people according to the FBI. The U.S. population at the time exceeded 323 million people.

Using the UCR's Index Crimes and Metropolitan Statistical Areas (MSA), we can estimate which Georgia cities and their surrounding counties experience violent crime offenses that exceeded the national average.

The areas which experienced violent crime offenses higher than the national average of 386.3 include:

1. Albany - 718.3

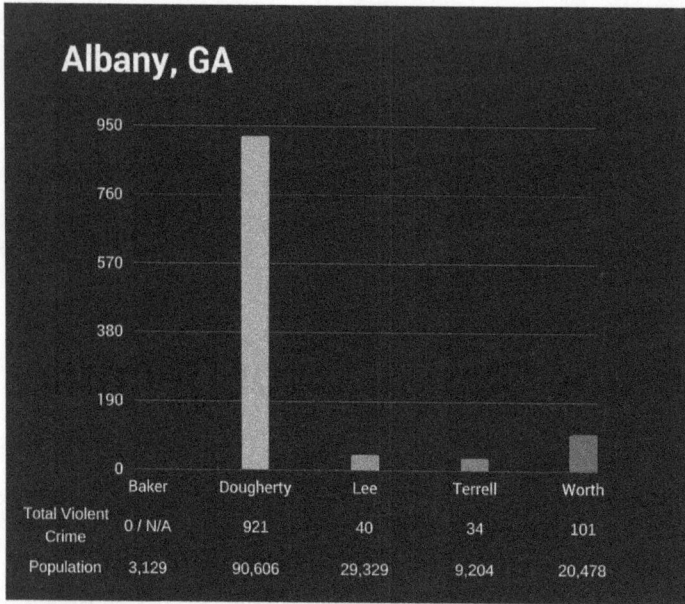

Albany, GA

	Baker	Dougherty	Lee	Terrell	Worth
Total Violent Crime	0 / N/A	921	40	34	101
Population	3,129	90,606	29,329	9,204	20,478

2. Columbus - 463.1

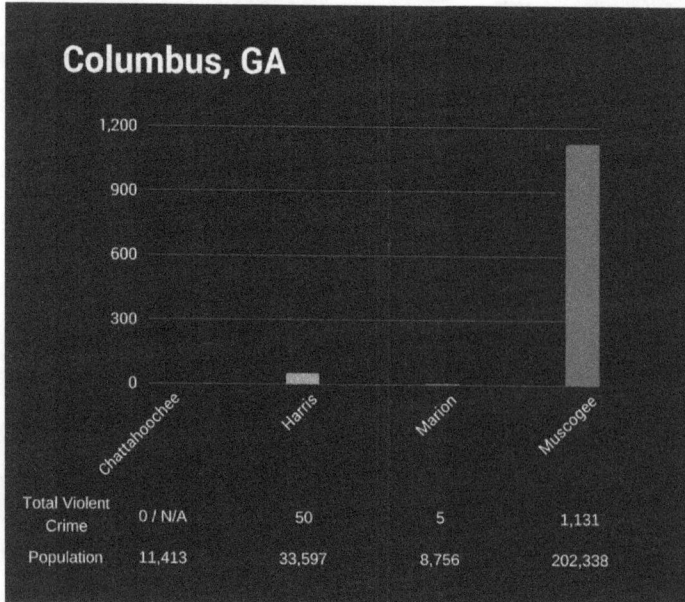

Columbus, GA

	Chattahoochee	Harris	Marion	Muscogee
Total Violent Crime	0 / N/A	50	5	1,131
Population	11,413	33,597	8,756	202,338

3. Warner Robins - 435.4

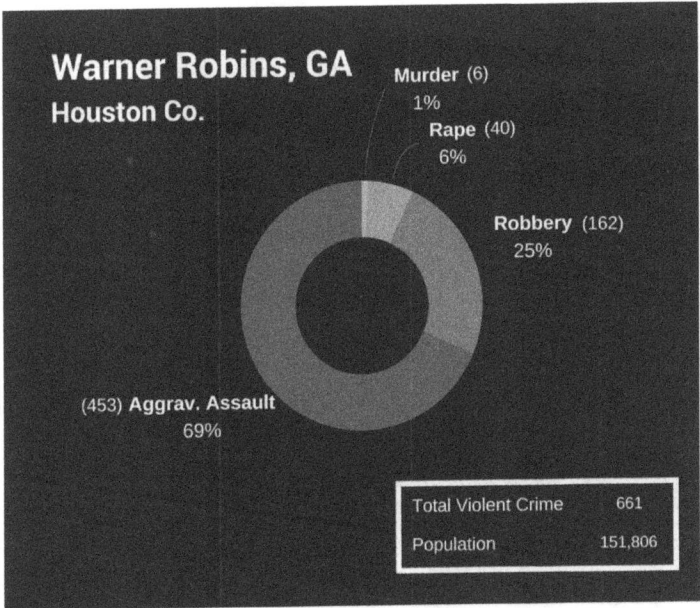

Warner Robins, GA
Houston Co.

Murder (6)
1%

Rape (40)
6%

Robbery (162)
25%

(453) Aggrav. Assault
69%

Total Violent Crime	661
Population	151,806

4. Hinesville - 425.9

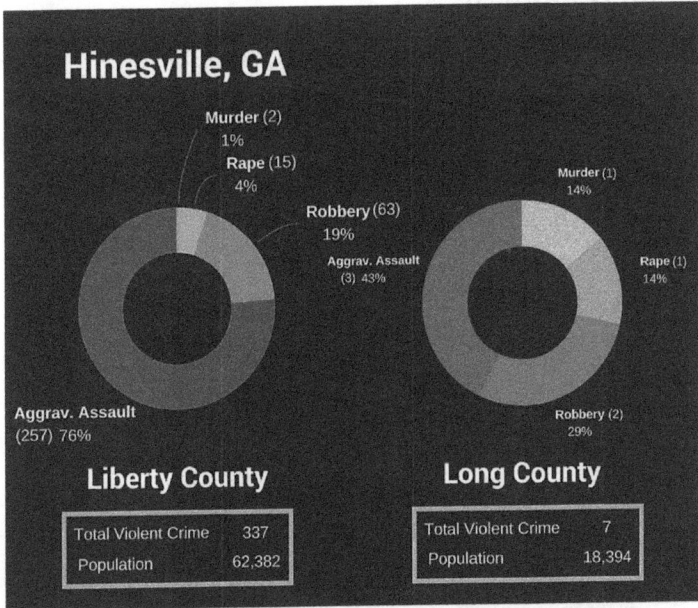

Hinesville, GA

Murder (2)
1%

Rape (15)
4%

Robbery (63)
19%

Aggrav. Assault
(3) 43%

Murder (1)
14%

Rape (1)
14%

Aggrav. Assault
(257) 76%

Robbery (2)
29%

Liberty County

Total Violent Crime	337
Population	62,382

Long County

Total Violent Crime	7
Population	18,394

5. Savannah - 417.4

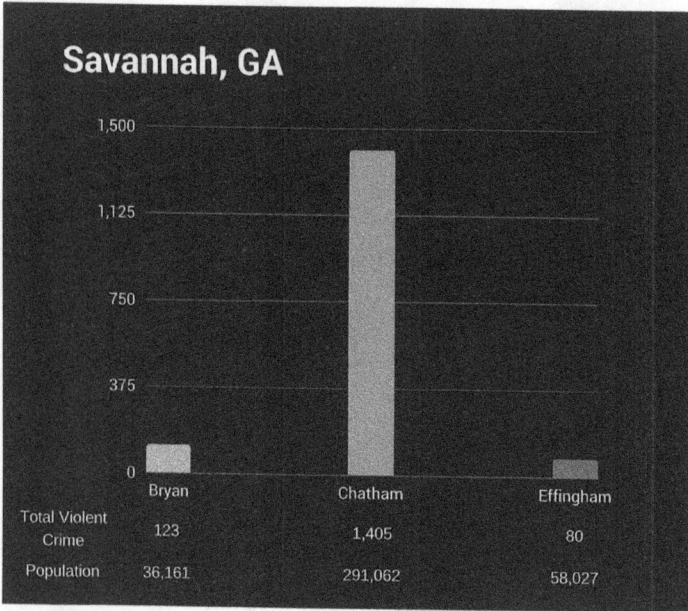

	Bryan	Chatham	Effingham
Total Violent Crime	123	1,405	80
Population	36,161	291,062	58,027

6. Atlanta - 406.5
(Bartow - Fulton Counties)

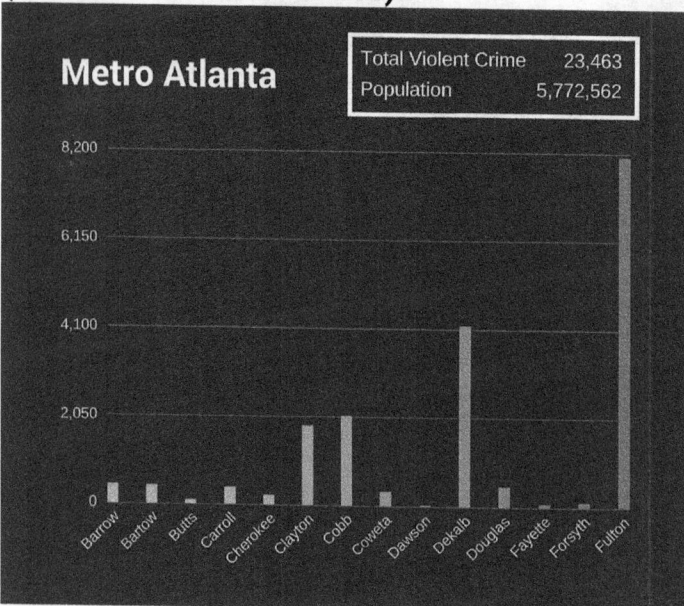

Total Violent Crime	23,463
Population	5,772,562

(Gwinnett - Walton Counties)

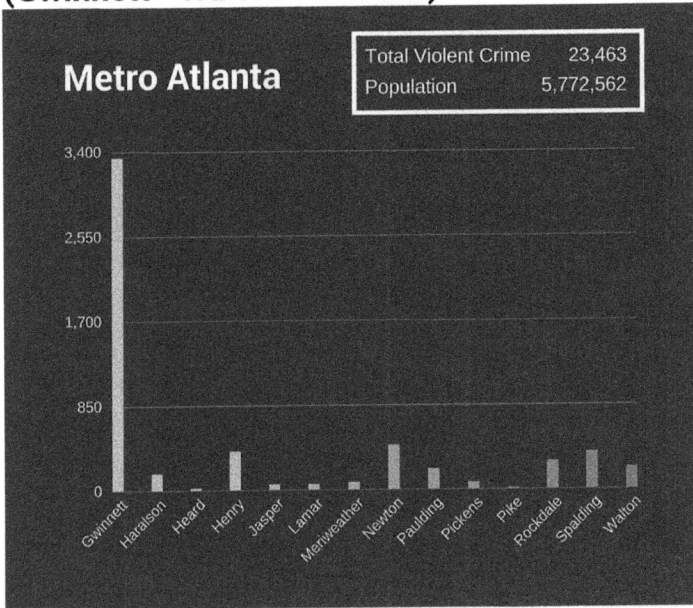

The Georgia cities and their surrounding counties that experienced fewer violent crime offenses than the national average in 2016 include:

- Macon - 379.6
- Brunswick - 372.2
- Dalton - 338.4
- Athens - 334.6
- Rome - 327.7
- Valdosta - 318.9
- Augusta - 282.8
- Gainesville - 259
- Chattanooga - 210.8

The good news is that while the statistics seem grim, the violent crime rate is still lower than it was a decade ago in 2007. In fact, the violent crime rate for Georgia overall is less than the national average -- about 377 offenses per 100,000 people. However, it's still important to take precautionary steps to keep you and your loved ones safe.

Here are three basic steps you can take right now:

1. Be vigilant when you are out and about. Put the cell phone away, take the headphones off when you are walking on the sidewalk, in parking lots, or going to and from your car. The bad guys are looking for easy victims and they are less likely to attack someone that is aware of their surroundings.

2. The buddy system doesn't just apply to pool safety. It also applies when you are out and about. When you are with another person or a group of people, you are less likely to be a target.

3. Have your keys in your hand when walking to your car. This will allow you to quickly get in, lock the doors, start the car, and drive off. You don't want to be searching through your purse or pockets while walking to your car.

References:

https://gbi.georgia.gov/crime-statistics

https://www.fbi.gov/news/pressrel/press-releases/fbi-releases-2016-crime-statistics

About the Author

Gary Martin Hays is an attorney with over 29 years of experience handling personal injury, wrongful death, workers' compensation, inadequate security, and social security disability claims in Georgia.

A former insurance defense lawyer, he now only represents injured victims and their families. Since starting his own firm in 1993, he has helped over 39,000 clients get the medical treatment and compensation they deserved.

Gary Martin Hays' legal accomplishments include being a member of the prestigious Multi-Million Dollar Advocates Forum, a society limited to attorneys who have received a settlement or verdict of at least $2 million dollars.

He has been recognized as a "Super Lawyer" by Atlanta Magazine as one of Georgia's top workers' compensation lawyers; as one of the Top 100 Trial Lawyers in Georgia since 2007 by the American Trial Lawyers' Association; and as one of the leading Plaintiffs' Lawyers in America by Lawdragon.

Gary is a 13-time best-selling author and co-author, including the #1 best-selling legal books: *The Authority on Personal Injury Claims in Georgia* and *The Authority on Workers' Compensation Claims in Georgia*.

www.ingramcontent.com/pod-product-compliance
Lightning Source LLC
Chambersburg PA
CBHW070410200326
41518CB00011B/2135

* 9 7 8 0 9 9 6 2 8 7 5 8 6 *